I-FREETHINK

THE IDEA GENERATION

ASHISH CHAHAL

ISBN 979-888530848-9

This book is dedicated all those people who have helped and supported me over the years...knowingly or unknowingly.

Contents

Contents

Preface

Be it Wealth, Success, Power, or Spirituality, everything is one. The objective of this book is to unlock the key to free minds. To challenge ourselves to open our thinking and allow creativity to thrive. In today's complex world we can often be limited by the cages of our own making. We take a direct and hard look at our everyday world, and invite the reader to explore where we could be missing the point, and challenge established norms.

Acknowledgements

I would like to thank everyone who has contributed to my life over the years knowingly...or unknowingly. My family, my teachers, colleagues, friends, fellow students, and my relatives. All the precious moments that meant so much.

Prologue

Be it Power, Business, or Society...we all need a break. Where are we...and where are we headed? Clarity is the need of the hour....confusion is rampant. In this book we offer the reader perspective that can help clear the mind towards new horizons. (www.i-freethink.com)

CHAPTER ONE

THE LIGHT WITHIN US

It is said that there is a light within all of us. This light is the light of our inner soul and a source of all strength, compassion, wisdom, knowledge, and joy. This light can show us the way when we are lost. It may also hold the key to being fearless. It may be extremely important to reach out to this amazing source, and maintain a constant connection to it.

For those who strike the connection with this light through effort or accident nothing would seem impossible. But how can we ensure a constant connection with this light, strengthen it, and allow it to guide us? To do so we must see with soft eyes which are not hardened with the desires of modern life. This connection can be crucial to living the life we want to live.

Connection to this light gives us courage, and allows us to have impact no matter what we do. Assume for instance that allowing our inner values to play out is causing us to risk losing control of a situation, or expose us in a way that may leave us vulnerable. This is certainly not advisable. So how do we find an ideal balance? The key may lie in drawing boundaries and being flexible, allowing our inner light to guide us, but constantly adapting against being vulnerable.

Constant adaption can allow us to stay flexible enough to stay in-charge of the situation. Hence it may be extremely important to be aware of our own internal makeup so that consistent behaviour can flow automatically. Ideally there should be no conflict between our inner values, and their honest expression in our work and lives, leading to consistency. The result can be a strong impact on our surroundings.

But is this ever so? Today's complexities dictate that we draw a line between these concepts, and maintain a duality with the notion that such integration may not be possible, or practical. It should be explored if this is indeed true.

Some good examples include Mahatma Gandhi, Mother Teresa, Nelson Mandela, Martin Luther King, and even Barack Obama. These were people who led with a clear vision which emanated from consistent inner values.

CHAPTER TWO

INSPIRATION

The idea that heightened inspiration and the ability to live an inspired life that touches people is alluring. The key may be to take life as it comes. For that we need to connect with the moments of our life. To be a receiver of the flows of life, fluid enough to accept its curves without letting them dislodge our existence. As uplifting as inspiration is, the downside can also be true. Uninspired effort can struggle even to make par. The same individual may appear to be a shadow of their own selves when uninspired. History is replete with examples of great achievers struggling to even survive through their uninspired patches of life. So how do we achieve this wonderful feat?

Seeking inspiration in silence....

Inspiration can spring from the ability to perceive and be empowered by seemingly ordinary things which within themselves hold a greater and a simple truth, and the ability to move the soul. An inspired moment can alter how we think and shape our life. As uplifting as inspiration is, the downside can also be true. Uninspired effort can struggle even to make par. The same individual may appear to be a shadow of their own selves when uninspired. History is replete with examples of great achievers struggling to even survive through their uninspired patches of life.

Inspiration is all around, but we need to tune in. To empty the mind. The key may lie in developing the ability to constantly seek and draw strength from everyday events. The greatest inspiration can also be to strive to inspire. There are many who claim that we should strive to make a difference. To be all we can be. If we think about it, striving implies a tendency towards what we are not, indicating a feeling of being inadequate. But maybe we should instead be all we are today. It may be important to realize that our very existence with our innate qualities does make a difference...whether we are aware of it or not.

If we think about it, no one can go through life without making a difference. Maybe we can take consolation in this to ease the pressure of always striving for something. This awareness can lead us to strive higher, without feeling the pressure of failure. And that really is what matters. What we need don't we, to not be afraid to fail?

To be or not to be...

In today's world we are hammered with external stimulus goading us with motivational quotes such as "just do it", "follow your dreams", etc. All this motivational energy can be very intimidating sometimes. The strongest motivation may be internal. Dreams can be mental projections with a promise of something in the future. We fight for our dream which involves belief, which can then become the root of conflict. The more powerful a dream the deeper the conflict. India-Pakistan conflict killed so many people because of conflicting dreams.

A blind man's dream is to see. But all those that can see, are they living their dream? When we have something, we dream of what we do not have. And then we desire it. And then when that is threatened, we fight. Then negativity sets in and the dream does not happen. Then we become discontent. Then we hate everyone. Till what we have is taken away. Then we become remorseful. And thus, the cycle continues. One way to fix this could be to be fully in the present. The thought that it may be fine to do nothing. Because we will stop doing nothing when we don't want to any more. The time will come.

Best motivation could be inner motivation. When we really want something badly, we will make it happen. No one would need to motivate us. I don't think someone screaming down our throat to achieve something is motivating. It could be the opposite. It's a thought. Instead of pushing ourselves constantly, which can create mental fatigue, allow the not pushing to eventually start pushing. Allow the 'not be' to bring forth the 'be'.

Seeking Inspiration...

Why do we at times loose inspiration? Let us explore this. We sometimes experience moments of great inspiration, which can then lead us to want to capture those inspired moments. Would it not be amazing to live constantly in this inspired mould? But can we really capture moments? Inspiration can even lead to attachment to the inspired energy. And attachment can be the enemy of inspiration, as inspiration often happens within freedom. So, the key then may seem to be detachment. To be free in the mind and soul.

Loneliness vs Aloneness...

Inspiration is all around but our mind needs to be de-cluttered, and our heart needs to be pure to connect with this inspired energy. The key then may be to understand the concept of aloneness vs loneliness. There lies a void within each of us which we try to run from through entertainment, distractions, and keeping busy. We fear being alone. But if we strike a relationship with our loneliness it can become aloneness, which is our gift and a great reservoir of creativity. It's also our connection with a higher power. Herein can lie our inspiration and our source of fearlessness.

CHAPTER THREE

PLANNING VS SPONTENIETY

Two extremely diverse yet equally compelling approaches to life could be one where we plan things in advance, vs one where we apply a spontaneous approach to life. Both have their pitfalls and advantages. Planning can go haywire through events which may be unforeseen. Recent wars and epidemics made people lose their homes, savings, and security which they had built over decades of planning. All wiped out in one go. Planning can give us a false sense of security that things will fall in place, and may leave us vulnerable if they don't.

Spontaneity on the other hand allows for dealing with life on a day by day and year by year basis, maybe even hour by hour. People who are spontaneous are comfortable with the unpredictability of life and can use it to their advantage to propel themselves higher.

Spontaneity offers the advantage of riding the potent energy of the constantly changing curves of life which planning can stifle. Ideally, we can strive to find the correct balance and follow a plan but keep it flexible enough for spontaneity to thrive. If there is no plan then when unpredictable things happen, we may have no plan to reshuffle and it can be total chaos. It's a battle many fight. In my view planning can be presumptuous that we understand the mystical forces of the universe which we often do not. So, the key here to rise to our potential may be to learn to ride these mystical forces.

But first we need to understand and bow down to the simple fact that we may not be in control of our lives, and that higher forces may be in control. But we can wield limited control, and we must. Yet stay flexible and nimble enough that our need for control does not stifle our observation of the truth, especially when we need to change course and accept what we cannot control. When things don't go as per plan, we should not feel paralyzed and unable to act. This would be possible if our mental structures are sound but nature flexible. The ability to function even if our belief system collapses could be very important, but very difficult. Most people draw strength and direction from their beliefs.

CHAPTER FOUR

BEING BUSY

It may be time to stop to think how important is it to be busy? Well, almost everyone in today's time wants to appear busy. If we are not busy, we may not be worthy members of society. Is it so? What would we do, if we stopped and started doing nothing? Of course, I am speaking about reasonable normal people. Doing nothing can empty the cup. How long would we do nothing? At some point would we not get up and say, enough is enough, I need to do something! What would that be? Maybe it would be what we want to do most. Although few would disengage from their busy schedule but nature seems to have a way. Covid anyone?

Sometimes the best things can happen to us when we stop being busy. Maybe we are too busy to love life. Again, being busy could be important once we have gone through a cycle of introspection. Being busy doing what we really want to do could be great. It would certainly be worth striving for. But how often have we been busy doing something, but at the back of our minds we know it's really not what we want? This then may be a bigger risk than all others!

CHAPTER FIVE

TRUTH

It is important to have a firm grasp of the truth at all times. Truth may be defined as what is closest to our reality, truth may also be subjective, but the truth we are referring to here is the honest assessment and understanding of the principles that govern our life and our environment. It's about having a very firm grip on the variables that make up our life and the ability to constantly keep pace with it. A famous Buddhist fable has a junior monk asking a master....'why is everything not perfect'? The Master replies...'But it is!". Meaning it may all be in our outlook. If we are right on the inside, everything outside also seems right.
Another famous saying goes that 'it is what it is'. This means that when we confront the truth it should be without bias, and hampered objectivity. Seeing clearly is intelligent. That is neither good nor bad. When a dumb person acknowledges that he is dumb, that is intelligent. If he consistently recognizes this, that can be an awakening.

Let us for a moment imagine that all our desires and needs at a moment in time are met. For a moment think about your life and everything you want from it. What if it magically came true? What if everything you ever wanted comes true and now you were still faced with the prospect of living out the rest of your life.

In truth you might become a different person and all of a sudden you would have a whole new set of wants and needs. But these might be of an entirely different nature, and more attuned with your real self, and could even be a lot more selfless...if that's you. So it might be worth a thought whether our current circumstances in terms of our immediate wants and needs might be keeping us from recognizing our true self and truly who we are to ourselves and others.

To illustrate this point we could narrate the story of the Buddha who had all the worldly pleasures and left them in search of enlightenment. Would he have done so if he did not have everything as a prince? Can you give up something which you do not have? If he did not have money he may have spent his entire life chasing money and power like everyone else instead of chasing the truth.

CHAPTER SIX

SEEKING TRUTH AND THE TWO MINDS

So, the big question: How do we understand and see the truth for what it is? The key here may lie in understanding the concept of the higher mind and the lower mind. The higher mind is our predisposition in life. It is an area of the mind which is omni-present and stores knowledge of our past experiences, and maybe even past lives. It is in sync with universal truth and conscience. Our lower mind is through which we function on a daily basis, and can easily get buried in the noise of our lives. This may be the duality of our existence.

All would agree that one very important purpose of our life may be to live fully, and minimize this duality to be in sync with our true selves. So how can we accomplish this great task? The answer may lie in hard work and sincerity. When we sincerely work on something with extreme amount of focus and conviction, we may reach a point where this duality can diminish. The gap between the two dimensions decreases and we can experience deep peace and satisfaction. It's also through this process where we can begin to understand and see what is through all the perception.

A lot of the world we live in is made up of perception, perspectives, image, reputation etc. We learn to perceive ourselves and others the way the world perceives us. This extreme could often lead to a life not of our own choosing but of managing one's expectations of others and vice-versa. Although it may hold some merit and acceptance by society, it can lead to a person getting lost as to their genuine self.

On the contrary if we lead our life as per our truth then acceptance could take longer but it eventually would happen. But we would have lived in harmony with our nature, which can be an extremely powerful way of being. And such a strong approach is this that whether acceptance happens or not, it may stop to matter. This can be greatly liberating.

CHAPTER SEVEN

SOCIETY

Are we saying that it is time to reconsider the assumptions our society is currently functioning under, or are we saying that it may always be time to reconsider the assumptions society is functioning under? The latter perhaps. The real way forward may be to understand the trappings of religion, which could be one of the strongest fabrics of society today.

When we become religious, we transfer power to a higher authority. We say oh God please make sure I am going to be ok; I am doing so much to make sure you are happy with me, and make sure I am going to be ok. Well, why do we need that assurance? It may be time to reconsider what we are afraid of. Are we ready to become fearless?

Maybe we should not worry about whether God is happy with us, and start thinking about whether 'we' are happy with us. Do we understand the root cause of our fear, and are we ready to eradicate it? It may be time to face our fears. And becoming fearless needs an understanding of our fears. We may need to make necessary adjustments to our life, and create a life of stronger conviction and a sustainable pace. Seeing our fears in correct light might be the first step in dissolving them. This brings me back to the earlier point about honesty.

CHAPTER EIGHT

CONFLICT

One of the key challenges of life also seems to be a conflict of interest. Our goals conflict, our relationships conflict, our priorities conflict, our personalities conflict, our actions conflict, even our thoughts conflict. So how do we live peacefully and yet achieve our goals? We may need to look at the seeds of conflict within our own self.

The beginning of external peace can spring from internal peace. Are we at peace? Do our internal goals coexist in a manner leading to fulfilment? We live in a world of constant flux. How can we be in constant connection with this flux? Be one with it? These seem to be important questions. The key here might be to integrate ourselves. So, what is the challenge of integrating ourselves?

Integration involves cohesion of motives, and living a life which may be in sync with our true nature. For instance, if we believe in equal opportunity, equal rights, and fairness, then in our jobs we could practice this concept. This may be an idealistic example, but on a practical level if our belief system is in direct opposition with our profession, or the manner in which we execute our duties, then over time this can lead to internal and external friction. This is often so. Today's complexities dictate that we draw a line between these concepts and maintain a duality, with the notion that such integration may not be possible. It should be explored whether this is indeed true.

Another Buddhist fable has two monks returning to their monastery. They pass a donkey at a distance. The donkey has a reputation for kicking. One of the monks known for his martial arts skill ventures close to the donkey to test the donkey's reputation. Sure enough the donkey kicks and the monk skilfully avoids the kicks and returns to the first monk. Pleased with himself and expecting his friend to be impressed, he then turns to the first monk and asks 'so what did you think?' The first monk says 'I thought would it not be nice if people all over the world stayed away from donkeys instead of fighting with them?'

As avoidable as conflict is, it is still a reality of today's world. It might be worth considering that power in a conflict can come from non-conflict. As in aggression emerging from non-aggression. Power can come from the non-physical such as peace in the heart and mind, and a oneness with the conflict and the opponent. Duality reduces power. 'I want to win' has 'I' which is ego, and 'want' which is desire. Both of which can block optimum performance, which may increase the chance of failure. As opposed to: "I am one with this conflict". 'I am having an experience which I can grow from". The result of victory or defeat lie in the future, and if we are rooted in the present then we don't allow our mind to go into the future.

There is a lot of romanticism attached to "fighting" these days. It's often exciting to watch glamorous heroes fighting it out on screen...eager to rip off their shirt and show their 6 packs abs and fighting skills. And a young impressionable person could be eager to show his or her 'stuff'. This eagerness can lead a person be a loose cannon so to speak.... a loaded gun-trigger happy and eager to go off at the slightest instigation, exposing a tendency to prove themselves....an insecurity maybe arising from feeling inadequate, and inner complexes which may lead to poor judgment. So then we have a trigger-happy young person with abundant energy, poor judgment, and quite possibly trained with lethal skills. Disaster in the making anyone?

The key then could be the principal of holding back. Non-conflict should be the priority then, not vice versa. This can be the check and measure to avoid disasters. Conflict when non-conflict is simply not an option anymore. A very powerful historical fable has the Buddha being confronted by a serial killer. After speaking to him with compassion the serial killer became a great disciple. Of-course the Buddha was God so he could pull it off. But most people would get their head chopped of...not recommended in extreme cases. But message here could be of the power of compassion which can dissolve many a volatile situation. It's just a tool but a very powerful one. Compassion can disarm the opponent off guard and lower their motivation to continue the conflict.

THE ROOT OF CONFLICT:

Conflict occurs when beliefs collide. How far would we go to protect a belief? Our beliefs make us who we are. If our belief is challenged, we fight to protect it. And this makes up our place in the world. People also fight because victory may have a reward which they desire. And this is in a nutshell one key root of conflict. Is there a way around it? Can we have higher perspective of our belief? Does one belief have to be wrong for one to be right? Can both beliefs be right? It may be important to reflect on this.

People also fight because victory may have a reward which they desire. Desire then also seems to be at the root of conflict. Some say life begins when we purge ourselves of all desire. It makes one wonder. Up until then.... what are we all doing? And what are we chasing? There we go. Maybe that's how we can get everything to chase us instead of always running after things.

CHAPTER NINE

CHANGE

One of the key challenges of life also seems to be a conflict of interest. Our goals conflict, our relationships conflict, our priorities conflict, our personalities conflict, our actions conflict, even our thoughts conflict. So how do we live peacefully and yet achieve our goals? We may need to look at the seeds of conflict within our own self.

The beginning of external peace can spring from internal peace. Are we at peace? Do our internal goals coexist in a manner leading to fulfilment? We live in a world of constant flux. How can we be in constant connection with this flux? Be one with it? These seem to be important questions. The key here might be to integrate ourselves. So, what is the challenge of integrating ourselves?

Integration involves cohesion of motives, and living a life which may be in sync with our true nature. For instance, if we believe in equal opportunity, equal rights, and fairness, then in our jobs we could practice this concept. This may be an idealistic example, but on a practical level if our belief system is in direct opposition with our profession, or the manner in which we execute our duties, then over time this can lead to internal and external friction. This is often so. Today's complexities dictate that we draw a line between these concepts and maintain a duality, with the notion that such integration may not be possible. It should be explored whether this is indeed true.

Another Buddhist fable has two monks returning to their monastery. They pass a donkey at a distance. The donkey has a reputation for kicking. One of the monks known for his martial arts skill ventures close to the donkey to test the donkey's reputation. Sure enough the donkey kicks and the monk skilfully avoids the kicks and returns to the first monk. Pleased with himself and expecting his friend to be impressed, he then turns to the first monk and asks 'so what did you think?' The first monk says 'I thought would it not be nice if people all over the world stayed away from donkeys instead of fighting with them?'

As avoidable as conflict is, it is still a reality of today's world. It might be worth considering that power in a conflict can come from non-conflict. As in aggression emerging from non-aggression. Power can come from the non-physical such as peace in the heart and mind, and a oneness with the conflict and the opponent. Duality reduces power. 'I want to win' has 'I' which is ego, and 'want' which is desire. Both of which can block optimum performance, which may increase the chance of failure. As opposed to: "I am one with this conflict". 'I am having an experience which I can grow from". The result of victory or defeat lie in the future, and if we are rooted in the present then we don't allow our mind to go into the future.

There is a lot of romanticism attached to "fighting" these days. It's often exciting to watch glamorous heroes fighting it out on screen...eager to rip off their shirt and show their 6 packs abs and fighting skills. And a young impressionable person could be eager to show his or her 'stuff'. This eagerness can lead a person be a loose cannon so to speak.... a loaded gun-trigger happy and eager to go off at the slightest instigation, exposing a tendency to prove themselves....an insecurity maybe arising from feeling inadequate, and inner complexes which may lead to poor judgment. So then we have a trigger-happy young person with abundant energy, poor judgment, and quite possibly trained with lethal skills. Disaster in the making anyone?

The key then could be the principal of holding back. Non-conflict should be the priority then, not vice versa. This can be the check and measure to avoid disasters. Conflict when non-conflict is simply not an option anymore. A very powerful historical fable has the Buddha being confronted by a serial killer. After speaking to him with compassion the serial killer became a great disciple. Of-course the Buddha was God so he could pull it off. But most people would get their head chopped of...not recommended in extreme cases. But message here could be of the power of compassion which can dissolve many a volatile situation. It's just a tool but a very powerful one. Compassion can disarm the opponent off guard and lower their motivation to continue the conflict.

THE ROOT OF CONFLICT:
Conflict occurs when beliefs collide. How far would we go to protect a belief? Our beliefs make us who we are. If our belief is challenged, we fight to protect it. And this makes up our place in the world. People also fight because victory may have a reward which they desire. And this is in a nutshell one key root of conflict. Is there a way around it? Can we have higher perspective of our belief? Does one belief have to be wrong for one to be right? Can both beliefs be right? It may be important to reflect on this.

People also fight because victory may have a reward which they desire. Desire then also seems to be at the root of conflict. Some say life begins when we purge ourselves of all desire. It makes one wonder. Up until then.... what are we all doing? And what are we chasing? There we go. Maybe that's how we can get everything to chase us instead of always running after things.

CHAPTER TEN

WEALTH

A great deal has been written about creating wealth, but a lot of books on wealth are about exactly that. Generating wealth by selling those books. So how do we generate wealth? Chasing money can simply be greed. One approach may be that the money should chase us. In-fact maybe we should not chase anything, everything should chase us. When we constantly chase, we may be blocking what is trying to come to us. Money, jobs, opportunities, etc. But how? I believe the most important thing may be insight.

Some would argue that it's about divine reflection. As in reflecting divine energies through spirituality, allowing us to be abundant within us, and attract everything we want. I am unsure about this. It could work for a while, but may put us at odds with the practical world. Divine grace and power can also enhance the I as in... I am so amazing, great, powerful etc. often leading to ego and duality. People often ask god for this and that which can put them back towards wants and desire. If a person feels content, he/she will never ask but get. God, spirituality, divinity may be great for unusual problems and hardship. But on a normal level, I think insight rules.

So we come back to insight. About our own self, and everything and everyone around us. Who are we and what do we have to offer the world? Insight can lead to recognizing prevalent truths around us. We live in a world of perception which can open up gaping holes where the truth may often get submerged. This can then show the way. Insight comes from an inquisitive mind. Always enquiring.

That's where true wealth may lie. Wealth is created around value, and Truth is value. The magic may happen when we simply don't have money in our thoughts. Thoughts about Money can create mental clutter and can block our energies. The truth is that there is no such thing as money. Money is manmade. There are simply needs. Money is little more than an idea. It's an illusion... So, if you think of money as an idea and not as a tangible asset, you will see that it takes nothing but an idea to obtain more money. Money was created simply to represent the power to satisfy one need for another to a least common and a measurable denominator. So we really need to develop the ability to understand needs, and our own ability to satisfy needs. Needs of others, of the market, and of ourselves.

CHAPTER ELEVEN

POWER

A great deal of thought today is often poured into the acquisition of power. Power play in life and corporate world is often seen as usual and required. Although there is a great deal of argument made in ancient texts that power should truly be applied for the upliftment of people and not suppression. But is this ever the case? Is this truly possible...or could this be a utopian goal? This may seem like an all-important question facing our country moving forward. If in fact this was followed, then Society would feel the positive impact very quickly. But the challenge may be to follow this from a practical viewpoint.

How can power be applied for upliftment and still be held on to? Holding on to power requires an individual to be self-centred. That is counterproductive, yet extremely important for moving forward. An answer to this could be the key for almost every step forward for our changing nation. How can we fight for power and not let it corrupt us? How can we hold on to influence and not be influenced by it? For that our mind and heart needs to be very clear as to our convictions, and why we may want and hold power. People often vie for power almost by default, maybe even for power's sake. The 'why' may not be so important. But it should be!

There are some people who think power may be compensation for low self-esteem. To feel better about themselves, to rise in their own eyes. This could be a dangerous combination. If you have such a person doing whatever to hold on to power, and then taking out personal grudges, then we have a big problem. In my belief power should not be used for personal grudges, but for constructive action...although that would need tremendous maturity. But motivation is motivation. Power is power. And people are people. Power corrupts and absolute power corrupts absolutely. When things get out of hand then nature has a way of stepping in. Covid anyone?

True power may also lie in having power over oneself. As with everything, one thought might be that we should not chase power, power should chase us. That would happen when the world needs what we have to offer, and to be at the right place at the right time where our convictions align up with the need of the hour. If we have the ability and willingness to do what needs to be done through balanced application, and few others do, then we will most likely succeed. But we need to be aware of our inner gifts.

CHAPTER TWELVE

PRIORITIES

Another important question may be one of priorities. How do we prioritize our life so as to create the right balance leading to brilliance? What is the ultimate priority which can lead the course of life in the right direction? Clearly our life must be directed by one overarching priority, or a set which drive us. It could be to create maximum value for self or society, or to help others, or to live life to the fullest, or to become really good at something, or to lead life by example. Or maybe quite simply whatever works.

Whatever works could be a powerful mantra in today's chaotic world. Although the problem may be that what happens when it stops working, and we cannot get out? Times change people change and needs change. As long as we are required, people are nice, warm, and welcoming. If we exist in a particular time and space where we are not really needed anymore, then all kind of problems spring up. There might be ego clashes, power struggles, and a constant need to continually prove ourselves. Meaning it may be time to move on.

The fallout of this concept could be that it might impede us from being part of sustained long-term relationships. After all if we frequently move on then we leave people behind. That may also not be so desirable. The key here could be that it's a moving target. We must be flexible enough, and adapt often enough, yet be open enough that there could be a lot for us beyond our immediate circumstances if we need to move on and break free of them.

CHAPTER THIRTEEN

RELIGION

Religion has a great influence on today's society. Religion involves following ideological beliefs, which if done in moderation can add a much-required dash of spirituality in our lives, leading to rejuvenation. But the problem is extremist thinking and dogmatism which can lead to extreme beliefs and hampered objectivity. Yet extremism seems to be here to stay. It has always existed, and it seems may always exist.

So obviously there must be a great deal supporting the existence of extremism. Maybe not something we can comprehend, but if it lives, then we must accept it. For acceptance can lead to understanding, which may lead to cure. Extremism implies that there is a central point which forms the basis of gauging what is extreme. But this differs from culture to culture. What is extreme for India may not be extreme for Pakistan if the focal point of the action lies in Pakistan.

Conversely, what is extreme for Pakistan may not be extreme for India if the origination point of the action lies in India. How much is too much? So how do we abstract away from it? How do we lead balanced lives where everything is done in the right spirit and to the right measure? Is it possible to see all of this as it was meant to be? Can we break out of the limitations holding us down and go beyond them, and yet not lose control? It almost seems that the right balance of a wild spirit and control may be the key to optimize our potential. Let us think this through.

First, we would need to understand what we need to live fully. We need the right temperament, and right attitude, and the ability to meet life head on. We need an objective set of values and an ability to comprehend the truth. But that is the point. Is there an absolute truth? Or does it differ from person to person? Truth may differ from person to person, but then there are some absolute truths which do hold the world together. It might be worthwhile examining what these are.

Religion is often times governed by religious books. The Qur'an, the Gita, and the Bible talk about similar concepts. But the question that springs to mind is that these books were written in prehistoric times, when no Internet existed, no telephones existed, and society was very different, and not as well connected as today.

Yet these books seem to influence our culture till today. It may be worth a thought that we could be living in the past. Don't these books in an innate sense contain potential for raw conflict, which may or may not express itself in a particular point in time?

Yet, conflict and violence rear their ugly head time and again. It could be a worthy effort to build bridges within these books creating room for compatibility and modernism. Our religions seem to be incompatible, and it might be time for higher compatibility. Building bridges between these great Holy books seem to hold some merit. We need to stop living in the past.

THE RELIGION PARADOX

It would be interesting to note that the leaders around who great religions are built were not religious. Jesus was not a religious man. Neither was Buddha. These were just influential people in history. But religions got built around them and these religions dictate money, power, and influence till today.

This could indeed be a paradox. Buddha gave up wealth, and a lot of people became wealthy later on by propagating his thinking. There is a huge statue of gold made in his honour in Thailand. This is quite a contradiction. What would the Buddha think about that?

CHAPTER FOURTEEN

SPIRITUALITY

There are as many theories on Spirituality as there are people. What is spirituality? In lay terms it could be defined as a realm which is slightly above the one we most commonly operate on. It's a fascinating subject with limitless potential if explored the correct way. It is said that we are spiritual beings having a human experience. Spirituality can connect us with our own immortality and our higher divine energies and purpose. It can give our life meaning and also give us a platform for connecting with other people. But the key here may seem to be applied spirituality. The ability to tap into spirituality to get what we want in life.

A common issue people often may face is why they have little of something and others have more. If a human went into depression that he cannot fly out like a bird, or if an elephant is sad that he cannot run like a horse, or a horse wants to be as big an elephant...then all life will always be depressed. The key here could be that we need to accept ourselves as a perfect divine creation and reflect divine energies. Then we will be abundant inside and outside and get everything we want. We must keep our egos in check though because divine reflection can be breathtakingly glorious. But notice that I said 'get what we want' as in what we need...not 'attract what we want'. Attract may imply power of attraction, which is what many people seem to overtly rely on today...especially celebrities if we notice.

Too much power of attraction can lead to imbalance, and cause disturbance of the energetic balance, which can come back to bite us. We can either be a part of the problem or part of the solution. We attract what we desire. And desire can be a snake. In spirituality some say that when we purge ourselves of all desire is when our life can truly begin. Scary thought.

If we stop to consider, it would seem that almost every high performing person in every field may have found some connection with spirituality. For it may be hard to go beyond a certain amount of effort and result without digging into spiritual strength. Spirituality cannot be delved into with conviction without eventually facing the important question of the existence of God.

There are as many theories of God as there are people in today's world. The truth is that although there is ample evidence of the existence of a higher power or powers, no one has seen God. God can sometimes be defined as the collective consciousness of Mankind. So it could be said that Man is God, or everyone's thinking taken together.

The other possibility could be that God may be an energy force which expresses itself in the form of Nature, and its gifts. Either way, it may be important to have some form of grasp on what God means to us, and how we can imbibe its significance within our lives. God may or may not exist, but certainly our lives are definitely governed by some higher principles, which tend to have a way of governing the general course of humanity. The closer we as people are in sync with these principles, the fuller our lives may tend to be in the long run. This is common wisdom.

These principles have exerted themselves over time and again, and may largely be responsible for restoring balance in the world, when balance may be disrupted. We have seen this in every walk of life, and every time something happens which mays not be in accordance with these principles; things eventually seem to even out. This can largely explain the credibility of the code, and the merits of sticking with this code even when inconvenient.

There is a fable about the Buddha being in hell before he was born as a prince. He was being driven by a tyrant who was making him and his partner ride the tyrant's chariot while being whipped. The Buddha could not see his partner's pain and jumped to protect him and take the whipping. This killed him and he was born a prince. This shows us how through compassion we can rise. (Don't try this at home) It is said that human life is an opportunity...a bridge. We can rise to higher beings through mindful and compassionate living or fall into the animal kingdom through animalistic behaviour in this life.

If we think about it in the universe three things are always a constant. The current moment, you, and the truth. Whether u are sitting in your room with a friend or u are sitting with God in heaven you are still you, the current moment is the current moment, and truth is still the truth. These three constants can define a lot of our existence no matter where we are. This can give us perspective on a lot about the afterlife.

CHAPTER FIFTEEN

EXISTENCE

Often, we may not be aware of our true frequency of existence. It's something which we may become aware of when some event happens in our life which forces us to face life at a level of reality which was not previously our plane of thinking. This sometimes happens accidentally like for instance a Near Death Experience (NDE). Often people who have gone through this type of an experience have reported how their entire take on life changed almost overnight, and that they became aware of a higher identity of their own self which they were not previously aware of.

This makes one wonder whether we go through our lives living in a manner which is not on even keel with our real self. The answer to this question could be extremely important since our life can present us with various options and choices which may need to be made in accordance with this self-awareness. A thoughtless approach to life can lead us to all sorts of complications. Although such an experience cannot be simulated or wished upon, but it does teach us to take life with a pinch of salt, and that we may not be truly operating on the level which may be authentic for us. And if this is true then rest assured, we will be jolted into this sooner or later.

This brings me back to my earlier point of rebuilding life from scratch. This knowledge could be key. For the closer we are to our reality, the closer we may be to making choices which could be correct for our future. In-fact it may not be a bad idea to give ourselves this jolt, although few would. In spirituality there is a concept of Kundalini which is the awakening of the inner serpent energy, which can be a pleasant energy if we are on our life path...but very destructive and painful if we may have strayed off course. In which case it jolts us and destroys the old life...and forces us to rebuild putting us on the right path.

CHAPTER SIXTEEN

HONESTY

Honesty is something we grapple with almost daily. Honesty springs from the inside, and can cause us harm if we let it go unchecked. It can expose us to others, and if not tactfully done, can put us on the wrong end of the things. As appealing as honesty is, the challenge in today's world does not seem to be how we can be honest, but how to appear honest. A lot of success in today's world stems from appearing a certain way as opposed to being a certain way. This can be an art more than a science. But yet, honesty in one's dealings and one's work will almost always be recognized and rewarded.

An artist of every kind will most certainly strive to find honesty in his work. The more honest a connection he has with his work, the more direct a connection of his work with his audience.

So how can we become more honest and yet insulate ourselves from harm? The answer may differ from person to person but would involve some level of detachment. Applied honesty with focused detachment and constant adaption. Drawing boundaries so to speak.

So how honest should we be? It may differ from person to person. I think an 80:20 rule could work well. More than 80% honesty can be an extreme, and the 20% would give room for movement. But the most important thing here may be to be honest with ourselves. Being in denial and seeing ourselves as we want to be and not as we are may lead to inconsistent behaviour, and mislead ourselves and others. It can also lead us to insecurities...and an inability to be internally secure, robbing us of our true destiny.

In life we will make mistakes, but honesty with self and others can minimize errors and keep us on the right path. But when mistakes do happen, then we may need to forgive ourselves and others. Easier said than done but important none the less. Forgiveness can be powerful, liberating, and internally cleansing. No matter how well we live life, we will err. Simply because our decisions may be based on a limited view with too many unknowns about higher dimensions.

CHAPTER SEVENTEEN

RISK

Risk and Reward go hand in hand, but so do Risk and Failure. Risk may involve taking a call which is not supported by evidence but with intuition, a hunch so to speak. Many a times we feel such intuition about something where we may be required to put a lot at stake. It's a bridge where many might take the safer route. This is what separates the risk takers from rest. It's a point where a risk taker would go with the intuition-based approach.

Let's delve into the mind of a risk taker for a second. A risk taker is often driven by his need to strive for higher potential and live a fuller life. A deeper belief in their potential, and an innate sense of their ability to bounce back if all hell broke loose often makes them more courageous. A risk taker also has a stronger grasp of their reality, and their own ability to call something which others might not be able to see, or believe in. It's also their confidence in their ability to walk on the edge, and experience life on a thin wire.

Conviction may be incredibly important here in terms of taking chances. Chances of a risk paying off in my understanding could be higher, if the conviction is extremely strong as to why we do something. If it's for a reason which propagates a good, then along with our own internal factors, higher universal factors may also go in our favour. Often times, when people take a risk, in their own minds they have the math figured out, and quite often they may not be taking a risk at all but playing to their potential.

Here the most important factor may be for the risk taker to have the ability to take the hit if things go wrong. Start with the assumption that things will fail. Then work backwards to eliminate points of failure. Here it might be worth considering that if we factor in the scenario that if things go wrong, we still gain then it could be a risk worth taking. For example, if a business fails unused goodwill can come in to play, which would never happen in good times which can be a waste. When we fall who will come to pick us up and who comes to do the opposite? And we would know real friends from enemies. A great insight.

CHAPTER EIGHTEEN

SEQUENCE OF LIFE

Sequential progression can amount to taking a sequential view of life. For instance, we are born, we gradually grow up, we get an education, we enter the work force, we get married, and have children so on and so forth. Normally we as human beings may be hard wired towards dealing with life best when it follows a sequence. Sequence lends predictability which can make it easier to predict, plan and execute for desired results. But what happens if this sequence is broken?

How would we deal with life if some of the sequence of events got disrupted and we had to restructure our lives? How would we measure up if we had an emotionally disturbing experience which made us rethink our priorities and take stock of our lives with new found realizations? This can occur due to tragedies, judgment errors etc. Sometimes macro events also cause great shifts in society disrupting patterns with which people live their lives. We faced this in recent times when the wars and recession took the world back 20 years. An answer to this dilemma may lie in understanding that life need not always be sequential.

How do we prepare ourselves for dealing with life if this sequence if broken? It may be important for us to be nimble enough to deal with whatever comes our way. We must recognize that the deeper meaning of life may lie beneath the structures we often build around our lives. The stereotypes we build and how we subconsciously defend these stereotypes even if they are wrong. We need to be aware of our own thinking, and develop the ability of switching to day-by-day mode as and when required. It's often when we are pushed into a corner into survival mode when each moment begins to matter.

CHAPTER NINETEEN

RANDOMNESS

Randomness is the opposite of sequential. This is when we recognize random events within our lives which have no real build-up making them unpredictable, but which eventually do form up towards a recognizable view point. Such events often point towards deeper mysteries of life, and can make for an interesting study.

For instance one of the most interesting and alluring things about falling in love is that it may happen completely out of the blue and purely random. Sometimes some people place so much premium on this chance event that they may end up restructuring their entire lives to allow this chance event to play itself out, often disrupting other relationships in place, and in turn crafting a whole new set of patterns. Other examples could include stumbling upon a chance formula for making money or making some other desirable activity happen.

Randomness is important since it can often play a great role in our lives, and if not taken into due consideration, can play havoc into our established way of functioning. People who become good at reading random events within their lives and treating them with proper attention can gain greatly from the hidden rewards from such events. Random can also be defined as the outcome of one's own actions and positioning which we may not have been previously aware of.

Some of the greatest discoveries in the world have happened randomly or by chance accident, and the people who were smart enough or attuned enough to capitalize on such events gained tremendously. It's also mastery of such events which can make life interesting, and infuse it with fresh perspective when required. The trouble with capitalizing randomness is that it can be so random that its unpredictability can make it that much harder to capitalize on. Random can also have immense power because random moves cannot be predicted by enemies. There are subtle shifts that are always happening around us and we need to be acutely aware of them to ride these waves.

This brings us to an extremely sought-after objective of human life. So sought after is it that many have happily given up their lives for this goal. But what is freedom? Let us enquire into this.

CHAPTER TWENTY

FREEDOM

Freedom can be defined as the ability and willingness to be able to exercise free will. To be able to do as one pleases, when one pleases. This could be to travel, to take time off from work, to meet with friends, and to choose a vocation of one's choice, etc. Freedom also involves being able to express oneself freely and without restraint, mostly within moral bounds, and without causing damage to society.

So why is this so important, and why does it hold such great significance and a premium towards our way of life? The answer may lie in the fact that unless we feel the freedom within our spirit, we cannot live up to our potential. Our life should be an honest reflection of ourselves. A free spirit can be infectious, and generate a feel-good factor, and an energy which radiates towards upliftment and achievement. Freedom can also be important to bring out the true potential of an individual, which can often spring from within the self, and may be beyond constraints. A free spirit understands spontaneity, and can capitalize the energy of random events.

So are we free? We live in a world of perceptions and expectations. We become what the world expects of us. Our bosses, our parents, our peers, etc. So how can we break free? We need to seek. We need to listen to our inner spirit. And we need to connect to our authentic self. Breaking free needs fearlessness, and to be fearless we need to connect to our inner light. We need to see the truth through the illusion. The truth can set us free.

CHAPTER TWENTY-ONE

TIME PAST PRESENT AND FUTURE

An intrinsic understanding of time may reveal that in truth, only the present exists. Past is a memory, and the future has not arrived yet. So, in an ideal view, a person should be completely rooted in the present, and have no projections about a future, and not be influenced by the past. This can be very tough, but not entirely impossible.

Being constantly present in the present can allow for immersion into one's own existence and oneness with the moments of our life. It can lead to a worry-free life where we don't get bogged down by the past, and constantly ponder about the future. Some future planning may always be required, but we should not allow our future to dictate our present, because it does not exist.

CHAPTER TWENTY-TWO

CHARACTER

An important but difficult to define ingredient to life is character. The common wisdom goes: when all else fails, character shines. Character involves a person's a set of values and attributes that he or she demonstrates time and again. In the initial stages when effort is put into developing this set of values, it may form an attitude. In later stages it could turn into character. A strong character can be a good cushion for the stumbling blocks in life.

The stronger the character, the stronger could be the response toward meeting these road blocks. It may be important to note here that a person may or may not be living his life in true accordance with his/her character. Sometimes they may not be aware of this duality, which can lead to frustration and conflict. In such times structural modifications within one's life may be necessary. It can also be an important aspect of failure, to bring forth the true character of a person.

CHAPTER TWENTY-THREE

GOOD V/S EVIL

Conventional wisdom says Good is virtue, and Evil may be violation of this virtue. But in today's time it is very tough to distinguish between the two. The balance keeps shifting. History is written by whoever wins. So who decides? The answer may lie in our own inner conscience. We always know. When we are on the side of the good, we feel good. When we are on the wrong, we may feel an inner conflict.

This brings us back to honesty with the self, and the importance of having a sound connection with oneself. We can always find a justification for doing something which violates a moral principal. But are we being honest with ourselves in such a scenario?

It could be that the ultimate judgment point is inner peace. People may talk about heaven and hell etc, but the truth is that Hell and Heaven can very much reside within us. Deep inner peace can be heavenly. Deep inner conflict and dissatisfaction could be Hell. This approach can make us mindful of living well in this life without illusions of the afterlife.

Having concepts and theories of the after-life can also lead us to being delusional since it may be a projection and quite possibly escapism. It can lead a person to create rules and an approach to life which may not have any basis in reality...with the theory of there being some form of judgment at a later date. This could lead to flawed thinking and decision making. It may be impossible to imagine something beyond our boundaries of thought and whatever we come up with might be wrong. So God, heaven, hell etc. may be mental projections which may not be true as we imagine them. Something might be there, but it's simply beyond us.

We must also look at evil with caution because evil can simply be a powerful and judgmental word as words can often skew perspectives. Sometimes an evil person may be evil because in his mind he is that good that he needs to be evil for balance, so it does not become an extreme. Everything could boil down to risk and the constantly changing dynamics of relationships. The game keeps changing and people may do bad things to stay in the game. What are you willing to put at stake for what you want in return? One could argue that a thief is not a thief till he gets caught. If he never gets caught, he is not a thief. A lot of people in the world live by this code. This is where character can keep us on course. A deeper set of unchanging rooted values which can guide us as to where to draw the line.

The truth is: everyone is playing a different game. If someone else's game cuts into ours to a point where it is harmful for us, he may be evil for us. There certainly are evil people in this world. But a lot of them may simply be normal people in circumstances beyond our understanding. We as people are hardwired for duality and binary thinking. We always think in terms of yes/no, good/bad, right/wrong, on/off...accept/reject etc. But so much of the world falls in between. We should be aware of the structures our mind falls into, and challenge ourselves to get outside our comfort zone to be objective and see the truth for what it is. It may be important to understand this if evil has to be fought.

CHAPTER TWENTY-FOUR

DISCIPLINE

No doubt discipline is extremely important for it can give structure to our activities. But sometimes in life it may also be important to allow discipline to fall, and we go through a phase where we have no discipline. This can achieve two things. One is that it can bring about a deep relaxation since it alleviates everything and helps one let loose so to speak.

The other advantage may be that slowly over time discipline can build itself back. But this might be of our liking, and a code we may be much more deeply comfortable with. So it will be discipline born out of our inherent nature, and not one we are pushed to adopt due to external pressure or circumstances.
If it's too hard, we are doing it wrong...

This is a great philosophical view, and goes to imply that we live the best life if we live without effort and yet strike the right balance. The notion that life is always full of problems and that we must always strive hard is a much-respected point of view in the world, but may not necessarily be true. If we do things in the right measure, then life can be effortless. If we are trying too hard towards something and it's not working, then maybe we are doing something wrong, and we could take a different approach.

CHAPTER TWENTY-FIVE

INNOVATION

As a world we have recently made a shift from an innovation driven world to a conflict driven world. This shift happened relatively quickly and the value previously being accorded to innovation went down drastically. In an innovation driven world, there is collaboration and trust towards building something new, taking the world forward. In an innovation driven world, failure has high tolerance, since to innovate one cannot be afraid to fail. So how do we make a shift from visionary experiments to practical survival? The key may lie in letting go and prioritizing to whatever works. By focusing on the positive we can take away the best from the innovative era.

Innovation can be above success and failure. Innovations change the world, and show people new direction, new thinking. But for one innovation which works, there may have to be innumerable failures. Our country and Society should build tolerance to failure. In a conflict driven world, the dynamics often change to power play and politics. Fault tolerance is much lower, stress levels are higher, and there is generally more negativity, conflict, and anger. We are seeing this now. Attitudes have shifted from broad to narrow, and all the innovations during the innovation era are going through practical absorption. This is fact. So, it may be extremely important to keep pace with the changing times and adjust one's life accordingly.

It may be a bitter pill to swallow for artists and innovators, and can be a crushing blow to their egos as innovators and artists often tend to indulge in their own grandiose. They may feel lost and confused and unable to function. It may be important for them to become more practical and applied, and to let go a bit and shift gears. Innovators can get attached to their ideas and attachment may lead to belief. So recent shifting times have taught us the importance of detachment from the fruits of our action.

Innovations hold promise, and promise points to future gratification which may never materialize.

CHAPTER TWENTY-SIX

OSCILLATION AND FLOAT

An interesting approach to stumble upon the building blocks of life is to allow yourself to oscillate freely, and 'float' to an extent. The gain is to develop the ability to recognize the winds, and the winds of change, and also to develop the ability to ride the winds of change. The risk may be to get lost at sea. This is again where relationships can help us stay on course. This may also be an extremely powerful approach to ride the mystical forces of spontaneity.

CHAPTER TWENTY-SEVEN

BUSINESS AS A TOOL OF SOCIETY

Business is often times looked upon as being all about money. This may be a massive oversimplification, and in my opinion an enticing invitation for getting lost in the jungle of greed. A better way to look at business might be to serve society for profit. If we look at the most successful businesses worldwide, they usually identified a pressing need in society very efficiently, and found a profitable way to fulfil that need over a sustained period of time.

A great example could be Walmart. Sam Walton identified the need for low-cost retail goods, and found a cost-effective way to fulfil that need. Let us think about it. If one identifies a real and a pressing need in society, and finds a cost effective and a profitable way to fulfil that need over a sustained period of time, how can one go wrong? This can keep things simple, and the conviction strong.

CHAPTER TWENTY-EIGHT

SHIVJI SNAKES AND FIBER OPTICS

Here's an interesting perspective on spirituality. India is a land of gods and goddesses. When one observes the world, we can see that a lot of things resemble snakes. The infrastructure like trains etc, fibre optic cables etc. Who controls all of this? It is said that Lord Shiva is the lord of darkness. It's very interesting to see how often we can observe the world around us and theorize the influence of such gods. In today's time one e-mail from the boss can break a person's career, and even his/her life. Is that not like being bitten by a deadly snake?

It could be a great exercise to observe things and relate them with supernatural dimensions. If we are lucky enough, we begin to observe certain patterns which may point us towards a breakthrough which we otherwise might not have made. A lot of great leaders and innovators have cited spiritual influence in finding their purpose and calling, including Steve Jobs who built Apple. Study of superstition and the paranormal can throw up interesting possibilities, if one is careful enough to stay on the right side of things and not fall into hearsay and dogma. Life can sometimes resemble a game of snakes and ladders. Shiva is often considered to be the lord of darkness. The connection to the light mentioned earlier could be our connection to this free-space, our connection to God, and to original creativity.

We need to get the focus back to the aspects which work and use them to one by one to recreate a winning combination. It's when a re-think may be required.

CHAPTER TWENTY-NINE

RELATIONSHIPS

We strike many relationships in life. And the science of relationships could be a complicated one. Some relationships work and some don't. So, what is the science behind relationships? It's also said that some souls move together from previous lives. We may even connect with people because there is a purpose we need to fulfil in their lives and vice versa. This purpose may reveal itself over time, and we would need time and patience to uncover this purpose.

Sometimes we progress in relationships to discover that down the line our relationships come together to move forward in tandem. This could indeed be an interesting and a marvellous discovery. It can be a lesson on acceptance. When we accept ourselves and our relationships, then may begin the journey of true fulfilment, and the discovery of one of the greatest purposes of life. The ability to extend cooperation to each other, and add value to the lives of others.

As with everything else, relationships also have a specific and measurable role in our lives, but can also add tremendous pain and heartache, as emotions get involved. One way to look at relationships could be that they are meant to log into our lives at the correct angles and dimensions, to add the value or correct measure of support and strength.

But if a relationship plugs into our life at an imbalanced tangent then it can wreak havoc and sometimes even topple us over. From this point of view, one can say that there may be no friends or enemies. Just relationships which need to plug in correctly to create the correct holistic picture of our lives. Many would disagree as there certainly are enemies but not as many as we might think.

So what happens when a relationship is bearing down too heavy on us or having a lopsided influence on us? Then a corrective measure may need to be taken. And this is where sometimes mistakes may happen. In an effort to correct or balance a relationship we must be careful not to shift blame or rejection. This could indeed be a tricky exercise. We come back to the mind's comfort zone of duality. Yes/No, Good/Bad, Accept/Reject. We may need to develop the ability to work with transitions.

Sensitivities and sentiments are harder to maintain than win over. Someone's feelings are easier to earn than to maintain. This lesson may be one of the greatest ones we learn as we progress in life. What I have observed is that if we give people space and freedom then it can be liberating and empowering. It's also liberating to not care about getting burdened with others feelings and sentiments. We cannot please everyone. But not caring comes with a price. I did not say not care about people. I said not care about getting burdened. When we really care about someone, we will do what matters when it matters. Because we will know when and how much.

CHAPTER THIRTY

SUCCESS

Although success is subjective one way to define it can be as follows:

The TPC Principal: Timing + Passion + Competence. In other words, a different perspective can be to meet a worthy goal in a noble manner to make a positive difference.

- Journey inwards and discover spiritual gifts and talents you may possess with which you can outshine others.
- Explore external environment and opportunities where these gifts may be most applicable for the higher good.
- Align yourself with these opportunities.
- Work Hard. Don't hold back.

Additionally, the following steps can also be followed to achieve the above result.
- Identify an objective

Take real stock of self-positioning, which could include:
- Connections
- Skill and Talent
- Opportunities
- Latent/Potent Energy
- Positioning
- Will
- Drive
- Motivation/Goals
- Alignment

So basically, take a good look at one's own existence and say...this is me. This entire gamut of attributes, features, and life's various dimensions making up my life. And then look at what it all sums up to. Throw it into the mix and recognize a worthy goal. This is what is possible. And then go after it without holding back. That almost seems to be the key then. Don't let anything come in the way. Don't question yourself. Once an objective is selected, don't hold back.

An extremely important challenge could be how do we maintain perspective on what is really important? How do we create a world which is rooted in true values and can give us a stronger platform for sustained achievement? It would almost seem that the most important ingredient is Freethink, which is the ability to question anything and everything with an open mind. True understanding can lead to true change. Would it not be wonderful if we lived a life of constant exploration...?

Speaking about extraordinary achievement, one thing to keep in mind here I think may be that water finds it's own balance and so do we as people. Some people rise to power as that may be their natural state....at that point in time. If we think about it, every soul seems to be vibrating on its own frequency, and will at some point find its space. Stars will become stars and superstars will become superstars as that's the vibration of their soul...at that point in time. And they may not be able to rest easy till they do. They will do whatever it takes to make it happen. And the universe will support it as it contributes to the balance of the universe...till it does not.

CHAPTER THIRTY-ONE

FAILURE

Let us for an instant examine what is failure? What is often seen as failure is but a combination of variables within and outside our control that may have played out differently from what we may have expected.

So presumably we fail. Things may not have gone our way because we fell short of giving it everything, or made errors of judgment. That aside, striving for what we could not achieve - on the face of it - may seem like a recipe for disaster. It is certainly not so, because within this may lie the secret to a greater success.

When desired results are not produced, our thinking and our way of functioning can come into question. Our very way of being is frowned upon and deemed to have failed. Failure is not tolerated well in today's fast paced society, which conveniently overlooks the fact that failure could be success in the making. It throws up an opportunity to re-evaluate our modus operandi, and can allow us to make adjustments and modifications accordingly.

It can be a painful experience no doubt, but in truth, we may learn a lot more from failure than success. Failure simply means we tried something beyond our ability which leads to growth. I would be very unsure of someone who always succeeds. It may mean they are only striving for what is within their ability. They may not experience personal growth.

Striving for something beyond our apparent reach could be the key to maximizing our potential - that x factor so to speak. The acceptance of society to tolerate the so-called failures in-fact can define the maturity of a country, and the eventual ability of individuals. Paradoxical as it may seem, the failures in our life can determine our path to a fuller life in the long run, as they strengthen our ability to deal with whatever life throws at us. Such a learning curve can cause immense growth, as opposed to a person who is mostly successful, but a total disaster when faced with smallest of failures. Therefore, failure can be a ladder to a greater success.

It's also during failure where our strongest supporters may come forward, which is an important advantage of failure, to gain a perspective of who is with us and who is not. Failure can re-introduce us to our limitations and the reality of the surroundings that we may be operating in, which can be critical for sustained progress in the long run. Some of the greatest discoveries in the world have also been accidental ones, and have fallen out of failures. I believe we should have a healthy relationship with failure. Good losers make good winners. We can't win them all. When we lose it's important to not become negative and start shifting blame and anger, or allow it to impact our self-esteem. Finding scapegoats and targeting people can have long term consequences. So a healthy self-esteem then may seem to be the key. To maintain objectivity.

Failure can also re-introduce us to our own abilities and inner potential which may be latent in good times. In short, we need to fail to gauge our mettle and what we are truly made up of. But we would need to protect ourselves from the opinions of others. Everyone has an opinion. But opinions clog our minds. After all, without an opinion, who are we? Don't our opinions make us who we are? Well, maybe...to an extent.

Let us think about this. What is an opinion? It's a perspective on something. And a shade of what we think something is or may be. But is it what it really is? Could we be biased? We are constantly hammered with a myriad of information from all sides. Are we unable to see something for what it really is, as opposed to what we want to see it as? This is something to consider. A skewed perspective or set of perspectives may lead to a skewed life. So how can we cut through this and live life more freely? We need to observe without bias and with objectivity.

CHAPTER THIRTY-TWO

YIELDING AND BOUNCING BACK

Yield is an important concept in dealing with unpredictable developments which are not working in our favour. If confrontation or opposition is not working, or may require too much disturbance of the existing balance, yielding could be an effective approach. Yielding is acceptance of a development, for the time being. It's like backing off from the source of trouble allowing the event to take its course. This gives us time to gain a better understanding of the situation. Once the force of the event softens, counter force can be applied to neutralize the damage.

BOUNCING BACK

What happens when we do everything right and things go wrong? The most important thing may be to prioritize. At times when we are at the top of our game we do a whole gamut of things and do them easily. But if we lose our stride, eve accomplishing half the number of things become a herculean challenge. This is where prioritizing plays an important role. We need to get the focus back to the aspects which work, and use them one by one to recreate a winning combination.

CHAPTER THIRTY-THREE

REBUILDING LIFE IN TIMES OF CHANGE

In recent times lives have been greatly disrupted. The shift from an innovation driven society to a conflict driven society has been a monumental and a sudden one. Imagine an entrepreneur who poured his heart and soul into an innovation driven risk suddenly found himself in the wrong end of a power struggle.

So how do we reconcile the two realities of our world? This has happened time and time again. Walt Disney encountered several such situations where his creations were snatched away from him before he finally came up with a business model around his creations.

The truth here I think is that at least once in our life we may need to rebuild our life from scratch. It could also be at this stage that we get a chance to gain a better assessment of ourselves, and the world around us. So how do we do it? How do we rebuild? The short answer may be that we do it one step at a time. Our experiences up until that point may have equipped us with all that we need to rebuild. But we need to trust ourselves through this phase. The most important thing here could be to stay positive and understand that what is happening may be good not bad. As we build life our strongest assets are often not visible to us. They may become visible when we reconstruct our life after it falls apart. So no matter how much we plan there could be a higher plan at work which might be way beyond us. So we need to bow down to this...even if it makes us uncomfortable that we are not in complete control. It can be the most humbling of all realities.

The most important basis for developing trust with ourselves during this phase could be to believe in ourselves. If we believe in us, it will most certainly show in our conviction.

CHAPTER THIRTY-FOUR

PATH TO SUCCESS

Meaningful achievements are often not comparative in nature, but one of reaching our own highest potential. Often times it may be the ability to allow ourselves to examine how we can accomplish something of significance. It would seem for sure that each one of us is blessed with some natural gift or a set of gifts. If we take a really hard look at these gifts, we might come up with one such gift which may stand out. So, if one comes up with a formula it could be something like this:

- Journey inwards to uncover such a gift. An ability to do something which stands out as an ability to shine in that specific area with ease. From a range of such gifts, pick the one that you have the maximum passion for or one which may be most required in the current times.
- Hone the talent to razor sharpness.- Explore the external environment as to where this talent could apply for maximum impact to make a positive difference
- Apply yourself. Work hard with discipline for consistent results.

Life gives us innumerable such opportunities to do incredible things, but we might not see them. Are we aware of the change that is constantly happening within ourselves? Our lives are jam packed with experience after experience and we may not get the time for some of these experiences to unfold, to allow us to feel the potent energy of these experiences. Sometimes if we stop at the right time, we may end up taking a giant leap. But we may not want to stop due to fear, fear that we will fall behind, and fear that we may be run over.

But how can we let fear dictate our lives? Action can be a great enabler for sure, and lead to results for certain, but we need to be sure that the motivator of that action is not fear. Action arising out of fear can at times lead us in the wrong direction. It almost seems to be a paradox; action may be required but not fear. Eradication of the fear can lead to the same act having greater significance. So being fearless may be the key. It also seems to be important to understand that we must not stop for the heck of it if we are in sync with the progress of our lives. But when the sync is off and a deeper and higher calling may want to present itself, then maybe we should.

CHAPTER THIRTY-FIVE

CONVICTION

Conviction could be one of the most important cornerstones of Success, if not the most important. Conviction can convert to belief which is strong enough for the effort to sail through the x zone, a zone where the tangible forces to take the effort through may be insufficient, and conviction can bind the effort together creating synergy towards reaching the ultimate destination.

Conviction might be rooted in a moral code, but may also just be a reason strong enough to pull all resources together. It could be a motive strong enough to see the project till the end. Why is the project or effort being undertaken, and what is the greater good that would come out of the effort? This could be at an individual level or a group level, or a community level.

CHAPTER THIRTY-SIX

GOD

How can any book on Freethinking be complete without speaking about God? The most important question: Is there a God?

Let us for a second question what we call God. An all-powerful being running the show? We have come up with forms and descriptions. But any such descriptions must be wrong. For how can we say God is beyond our comprehension and yet try to comprehend him? The concept of God was created by us. Which may mean that it's bound by our boundaries of thought. Yet we say God is beyond our thinking. This may be paradoxical and the logic negates itself. So there may be no God as we visualize him. And yet God works.

Time and again the concept of God has shown humanity the way. Faith makes us strong and gives us direction. But it could be that our own belief is giving us conviction which works the magic. Not God. And we already spoke about the power of conviction. So which is it? The question that may baffle some is that if God created everything then who created God?

That may seem to be an easy one. The question assumes that something may be outside God for it to create God. But God by definition is all pervading so it cannot have a creator. Otherwise, it would not be God. We could also say that everything is God. Because we often visualize God as a separate entity but since everything is one, everything is God. So all of existence is God. Matter and non-matter. So maybe there is no God as a separate entity. But if everyone wants one, he/she exists. Just like quantum particles exist if observed, God exists if worshiped.

But is someone running the show? Sure looks like it. We certainly do not seem to be in the hands of chance. Chance can account for a lot. But not everything. Evidence of divine will is difficult to ignore. For those big on evidence and honest seekers there almost seems to be more evidence of God than anything else in the universe.

Everywhere we look, the universe, the environment, personal experiences, books, movies, faith-based stories all point towards a creator who seems to like playing hide and seek with us. So we can maybe not see him but realize him. God has not been proven yet but God sometimes seems to be the most provable fact of the universe. But what is God? A process, energy, balance, cosmic intelligence, or a higher being? Maybe all of it. The truth is it's a question which cannot be answered only contemplated.

We have turned God into a mystery but God maybe the opposite of mystery. God is supreme truth and how can supreme truth be a mystery? A stone is a stone, sand is sand, God is god. For an Ant creating a software program is a big deal but not for a human. For us creating the universe is a big deal but not for God. It's all relative. Universe.Destroy or Universe.Create (100000) done!

CHAPTER THIRTY-SEVEN

OUR MORAL PLANE

Whether we like it or not, it would seem we all have a moral plane of functioning. A moral plane is one which we often use as a guiding mechanism for important decisions in life. If something important is at stake, would we lie for it? Would we steal to save a life? Would we marry someone for money? These are choices which not only dictate our lives but can dictate the lives of others as well.

So for a robust moral plane our inner values must be very firmly grounded because sometimes these choices may need to be made quickly. We must spend time reflecting deeply on our own authentic moral plane, for it should be one which comes naturally to us. Coming up with a wishful one can create tremendous confusion. It might even need a hit and try approach to see what we are all about. Of-course this can be modified based on personal experiences but that would need time and tremendous effort and motivation strong enough in which case we would do it anyway.

CHAPTER THIRTY-EIGHT

LOVE

A much sought after yet often misunderstood human desire. We seek love throughout our lives. Yet when we find it we can often be discontent. Why? The answer may lie in our concept of the 'I'. For a woman in a relationship, it can often be about her life, her home, her needs, her man, her ambitions, and so on and so forth. Same goes for the man. Expectations are high built up by films and media with models and actors looking like Greek gods taking on warlords single-handed.

All this can create a bubble of wants and desires leading to discontentment and conflicts. The answer may lie in shifting from the 'I' to the 'we'. It may also be important to not expect your partner to make you happy. The blatant truth is I think no one can make anyone happy. We may need to connect to our own inner happiness and share with a partner who has done the same. If one partner rides on the happiness of the other, then it can be a one-way street which may be unfair on the other person, and breed trouble and resentment for both. As for expecting a partner to take to take on warlords single-handed, we usually have trained experts for that. Heroes belong in films, and these days, they belong in jail!

CHAPTER THIRTY-NINE

FINITE LIFE, INFINITE POSSIBILITIES.

If we stop to give it some thought, our lives are finite, but the possibilities within our lives are infinite. So, it can be a battle of choices. But the very equation presents an interesting dilemma. We certainly cannot do it all. Even if we try. It means that our life may be hard wired for disappointment. No matter how much we do, we may eventually be disappointed. The sooner we recognize this fact the better. This realization can lead us to detachment from the results of our actions. So how do we strike the right balance? I guess we do the best we can.

For those who seek enlightenment, it can be a liberating thought that enlightenment may not be something to attain, but a realization that we may already be enlightened. How can we aspire for something we have never experienced? It can be mental projection. A concept of how an experience might be. And to desire it. It's said that enlightenment may be our spiritual destiny. To purge ourselves of all desire. So, we live in the moment, every moment...fully and completely. Either we get there through the process of life...after life after life till we have no desire. Or we make a choice now and take control of the destiny of our soul. Some also say that our life begins when we get rid of desire. Scary thought. Makes one wonder...up until then what are we all chasing?

Realization they say could be one of life's greatest treasures. Alexander realized towards the end of his life that all his wealth and power could not give him one additional day of life. He advised his followers against his way of life. It is said that his realizations made him Alexander the Great, not his conquests. Do we need to conquer half the world to reach this realization, or can we learn from the realizations of others who have been there and done that? Food for thought!

We live in a complex world of perceptions. We do what we do based on our understanding at that point of time. But it's not what we do consciously, but subconsciously that we sow. When someone is being good to others, the underlying sense of superiority or deception may be seen by others not themselves. It's what we don't see is what we sow and we reap, what we see we can manipulate. It's often why the people who we expect to be with us during tough times often disappear, and unexpected people may support us. 20 years later it might all look like a mistake anyway no matter what we do. So forgiveness then could become the key...of ourselves and others. Self-acceptance can be so powerful that it gives us the license to be us. To be free, and not bogged down by the fear of mistakes, and the future.
So how then do we find our happiness?

CHAPTER FORTY

HAPPINESS CREATIVITY AND BEING FEARLESS

We can concur from everyday experience that one key to life could be a basic foundation of happiness. The all elusive yet worthy goal to aspire for. Yet one which has dogged and confounded people in all walks of life. The theory of happiness and its importance was introduced in Buddhist thinking generations back. We are now in a time where the thinking might need to move beyond that.

Happiness now may no longer be a goal, but a foundation layer upon which a life of accomplishment could be built. We should stop to consider that accomplishment may not be the road to happiness, but vice-verse. Yet there are people who strive hard to accomplish great things hoping to reach a point where they will be happy.

This could be flawed thinking.
Building a life of accomplishment based on a happy predisposition can also make an individual unafraid. If in business or profession loss does occur, the individual may not be very deeply affected since their happiness would be intact. And if a person does find themselves in circumstances where their happiness is compromised, then it may be extremely important to make necessary adjustment to restore balance before too much damage is done, even if it means sacrificing accomplishment for a period of time. This could be extremely important.

In truth, when we look around, it often seems that all levels of creativity may have already been achieved. So how can we do something of meaning when so much amazing stuff is already happening all around us? Films,

Television, Advertising, and Sport have already touched superhuman levels of achievement. So how do we in all this madness make our contribution, without going crazy? One thought would be to try and go beyond it all. To pre-empt time. Time brings forth new horizons, and we need to be ahead of the curve. In a period of confusion, clarity could be the hottest commodity. Today clarity may be the need of the hour. Confusion is rampant.

Maybe we need not worry about what's happening around us and simply focus on what it is that we are designed for and meant for. For instance you might want to compete for a job but there may be too many competitors. So how to manage?

We should note that no matter how many competitors, there is usually only one right choice, and ideally that person knows it. Then compete. Otherwise, don't waste time. Unless you want the growth from the experience of competing, which could be a separate matter. Either ways you would know what you are getting out of it and will not be disappointed.

It is also said that there exists a deep and a basic void in each of us as a basic quality of human existence. This void is the void of loneliness or Aloneness depending on the outlook of the individual. Often activities in the world may be geared towards filling this void through distractions.

Advertisements and movies often address this void through colourful and smartly crafted messages enthralling the audience. Filling this void could be the very basic need of everyone, and one they would freely pay for. Often this void may also be the reason for some of our relationships. But the key may lie in our own connection with this void.

In truth the void may not the problem to run away from, but the reservoir of solutions. People fortunate enough to have made a direct and honest connection with this void through effort or accident may have chanced upon a powerful key to creativity, insight, and personal power. Making a direct and honest connection to this void can also allow us to draw from its vastness.

It can be a liberating revelation allowing a person to be fearless in pursuit of material or spiritual goals. For often times, it is this void which can be the source of fear. But if we confront it, it can become the source of courage. Fear of loneliness and isolation can cause people to do incredible things, or incredibly stupid things. It can swing both ways. Being fearless may be the key to living life fully.

But how can we be fearless and yet maintain a healthy balance towards practicality? How do we challenge boundaries and yet not allow ourselves to lose control? The answer may lie in having trusting relationships around us which help maintain the balance giving us perspective when we go astray. Relationships can be our guiding stars.

When we think about it, we can see that the world exists on various strata. Given today's marketing machinery and myriad of illusions and projections, it may not be very hard to see that people can exist on a level which may be far from the real world. By real world I mean a dimension which is independent of influence and projection. We can see how challenging this may be. So how do we ensure that we maintain the correct perspective in this situation? Influence and projection seem to be everywhere.

Companies, schools of thought, and all sorts of marketing literature seem to have mastered the art of convincing us of needs and possibilities which don't even exist. We are being sold at every turn of life without us even knowing it. So how can we see through all of this?

How can we root ourselves in reality to an extent that we become immune to all of this influence, and lead a life of real conviction....and insight? Success then becomes easier to achieve, since our thoughts and actions would be driven by a real and true grasp of our world around us, and not one that we are made to believe in. This may seem easier said than done, but in reality, can be extremely tough, since we are constantly barraged with marketing messages which often times appeal to our subconscious without us even being aware. So in turn we need a great deal of self-awareness to be aware of this phenomenon, and possess a filtering mechanism which can cut through all of this. This brings us back to the importance of insight.

Moving from a Micro to a Macro view, our culture is rooted in tradition, although we seem to be making rapid strides towards the future. But the key question could be...how important are our roots and how can we draw strength from them and not let them hold us back? This then may seem to be an all-important question: how do we find the right balance towards transforming from our traditional roots towards the future, and yet not forget our roots?

The past can show us the way forward, and the key may lie in making a seamless transition allowing both to coexist with each being the strength of the other. Our roots may be our biggest asset. This then could be our USP, the ability to draw strength from our roots and build a progressive future, but without allowing one to overwhelm the other. This can be a tough task, because in the tug of war one may often try to prevail over the other. It can be a great feat to have a fusion. But for this each generation will have to understand the other, and give respect, room, and space to the other.

9 798885 308489

Printed by Libri Plureos GmbH in Hamburg,
Germany